No I in Allen

Emily Allen

BookLeaf
Publishing

India | USA | UK

Presentation by *BookLeaf Publishing*

Web: www.bookleafpub.com

E-mail: info@bookleafpub.com

ISBN : 9789357447232

First edition 2021

DEDICATION

To Ben, Tommy, William, Max and Molly xxx

ACKNOWLEDGEMENT

Thank you firstly goes out to my best friend, Sophia. I started writing poems as a personal gift for her birthdays, hen do and wedding. Every single one she loved and gave me the confidence to try it for others.

Thank you also goes out to BookLeaf Publishing for giving me this opportunity to have a book of my own work.

PREFACE

They say write what you know well I decided to do just that. Being a mother changed my life, being a mother in lockdown and pregnant changed it all over again. My loves gave me the inspiration for these poems and for something they can read when they are older.

My Dear Body

My dear body you have changed
Two pregnancies, two amazing children
Two lots of eating for two when I shouldn't
Breastfeeding and tiredness, lockdowns and
tantrums
It's all caused you to gain weight

My dear body you have changed
Takeaways instead of a home cooked meal
Sitting on the sofa when I said I'd workout
Napping instead of walking, eating chocolate
instead of an apple
It's all caused you to not know the person in the
mirror

My dear body you have changed
A heart that can hold endless love
Arms that can stretch right round for a hug
Patience that can outlast the screams
A stomach that can hold even the worst smells
And hands to hold yours
It's all caused you to be an amazing mother

My dear body you have changed and it's been
worth it all

A Poem for You

Nearly 10 years we've been together
In a lot of ways it seems like forever
We met when we were still young
Going out, drinking and having fun
We're older now and have a family
Being a father, that's what makes you manly
I love you, I have definitely won the jackpot
Even when I have to nag you (a lot)
We are a team, support and strength
Even when we're not on the same wavelength
Here is to our future, old, saggy and grey
But for now, let's enjoy each and every day

We're All Invited to a Wedding

We're all invited to a wedding, looking forward
to celebrate
Oh, we're all invited to a wedding, two young
children, how will I celebrate?

I'm seeing old friends, I want to look good, but
I've put on weight from having kids
I'm seeing old friends, I can't wait for them to
meet the kids

It's the day, all outfits are ready, time to
coordinate getting dressed, the anxiety building,
trying not to be late
Everyone is ready, we're here, just in time,
anxiety easing, we weren't (that) late

The vows and the food, sit still, stay here, rock
to sleep
Time to toast the couple and grab a drink whilst
they're both asleep

Ah, here we go, it's time for the dancing, the
evening has started, the energy is thriving
Oh no, I have kids, time to head home, their
energy is dying

We were all invited to a wedding, we had fun
celebrating
We were all invited to a wedding, I don't
remember saying congratulations, or actually
celebrating

Max and Molly

Eight paws and two tails makes two cats
Life with cats is cuddles on their term
Feeling like sometimes you live in their house
Saying sorry to the bird or mouse you have to
put in the bin
Worrying at the yearly check up and booster
they're ok
Hoping that you won't leave when I bring home
the baby
Watching you peacefully sleep, seeing you
content
Feeling joyful that you feel peace here
Eight paws and two tails makes two cats

The World for You

You changed my world when you came into it
I said I'd change the world to make you happy
Now, now the world is changing and I worry
Violence, Brexit and the rich getting richer
The world itself is dying

I have to try and teach you so much stuff
Not just maths and colours, compassion and love
The world is changing and I'm trying to help
Stop eating meat, buy eco friendly, plant a tree
I hope the world is there when you're 33

You changed my world when you came into it
Now I have to stop the world changing for you
to live it

Just Another Day

I took you to the park today
Watched you laugh, slide and play
We got home and then you changed
Terrible twos, you just were outraged
You're learning to be independent, I'm proud
You're learning to talk and are so very loud
You're oh so sweet, kind and cheeky
But if you don't get your way, so shrieky
I'm learning to understand you more
But oh my days, I definitely almost swore
I took you to the park today
And if I could, I'd do it everyday

It's OK

Being a mum is hard, but you can't say that
Having children completes me, even when
they're a twat
Old friends want you to be the person before
But sometimes you really just want to shut the
door
Yes, I'd love to go out and drink and dance
But a hangover tomorrow, err no chance
I'll say hi and be social when I have the time
But mainly I want to watch Netflix or Prime
Torn between friends and finding an hour of
peace
When does this dilemma ever cease?
I guess I can be a mum and grieve being free
And now I'll go back to my cold tea

Autumn with a Toddler

The leaves turn orange, the rain comes down
All that means is a splashy playground
Seeing the fallen twigs and conkers
It's very wet now, I must be bonkers
Showing you nature and outdoor play
Because I'm not watching TV all day
You fell in the mud, you hurt your bum
Wet eyes, muddy hands and cried out mum
The leaves turn orange, the rain came down
We had fun in the splashy playground

Who will you be?

You're little now, you smile, you laugh, you cry
But I wonder who you'll be in a few years time
Will you cook and clean or just be a good guy?
Will you do the salt, shot and lime?

I wipe your tears (and your bum)
School, college, work and love
What will happen in years to come
Whatever it is, you, I'll be proud of

You're little now, you smile, you laugh, you cry
Who knows what you'll be in a few years time
But for now, know whatever you try
I'll love you forever, thanks for being mine

My Country

I was once proud to be English
The nature, the people and the heritage
I was once proud to be English
I am white and went to a private school
I was once proud to be English
I grew up and learned the truth

I am no longer proud to be English
The hate, the racism and the Torys
I am no longer proud to be English
The victim blaming and selfishness
I am no longer proud to be English
This isn't the country I knew

I want to be proud to be English
Embrace culture, refugees and sacrifice
I want to be proud to be English
Recycle, more nature and less capitalism
I want to be proud to be English
I hope we can all help the many not few

Mental Health

Stuck inside your mind with no escape
Thinking thoughts that are so wrong
Depression, ADHD, autism, suicide
Just some of the names attached
Mental Health is so important
But it's always taken for granted
So tell me friend, speak what's wrong
I'll try and talk first if you can't reach me
Just know you're never alone
I'll be inside your mind too and we will escape

Working Mum

Being back at work and being a mum
Juggling the time for errands and fun
Being on my own but thinking of you
Wondering if you're missing me too

Work is time to be an adult again
Feeling guilty for feeling zen
Peace and quiet just feels weird
It's like you've both disappeared

But a day off is coming up soon
So we can cuddle and watch a cartoon
I hope it's ok that I'm not here all the time
But extra cuddles for pick up and bedtime

To All My Friends

Dear friends, I'm sorry I don't text as much
I'm sorry I'm not out as much
I'm sorry for being a rubbish friend

Please don't think I don't love you anymore
Please don't think I don't want to hang anymore
Please don't think we've fallen out

I think about you all the time
I think about seeing you again
I think about whether 3 in the morning is too
early to message

You see, when I think about you, it's normally
really early and I don't want to bother you
When I think about you, I'm normally
bombarded with something new

I'll get better soon, I promise
But until then, please hang in there, being a
mum is hard

The Gym

I'm excited, I'm joining the gym again
It's been a year out, it feels like seeing a friend
To some its just a bunch of machines
To me, it's my free space (and get lean)
Feel the rush of endorphins when I'm done
Think hell yeah, I did it, that was actually fun

I never thought I'd miss being at the gym
I'd have definitely rather cut off a limb
But it's gives me head space to focus
And teaching the boys health is just a bonus
I'm excited, I'm joining the gym again

It's Friday Night

It's the Friday, the weekend is here
Used to be filled with dancing and beer
Then sleeping it off and doing it Saturday night
I hope my liver survived and has come out
alright

Now it's going to bed early and planning ahead
Long walks in the forest or playing in the park
Fridays have changed quite a bit
And I wouldn't change it, well maybe some to
babysit

Tick Tock

Two kids and chores to do
Cook, clean, cook, clean
The hours ticking away on the clock
No time to chill and if you do things pile up
A perfect house does not make a perfect place
Play, laughter and breathing fresh air
Teaching young minds about the world
The hours are ticking away on the clock
Embracing the cuddles now
The cleaning can wait for tomorrow

Not Her Fault

Don't walk late at night, not her fault
Don't walk alone, not her fault
Don't wear revealing clothes, not her fault
Victim blame, victim shame

Don't say boys being boys, taught behaviour
Don't say they were really drunk, not an excuse
Don't say he was wound up, go for a run instead
This can stop, when you blame him

Girl power is a movement like no other
Coming together to really show what happens
If you don't see it then you must ignorant
It's never her fault, stop the victim shame

Brothers

I could watch you both and smile all day
The way you laugh, giggle and play
A bond that's so pure, strong and bright
I know you there will be days where you fight
But I know you will always stay together
Because a brother's love is forever

Why Hate?

The world feels so dark and cold
Racism, sexism and killings untold
Why are people choosing this I hear
Because it's born out of desperation and fear

We stop darkness by showing compassion
By stopping poverty, wars and famine
The world has hope to be bright
I just hope we're strong for the fight

Relax

If you're reading this, breath in
Hold, keep holding, now out
Repeat again and then pour a gin
To relieve any self doubt

I hope that helped to ease your strain
Or try talking to someone and share the pain
Read this whenever you need a lift
Because I promise, the weight will shift

Sleep

Warm, comfy, and hugs just right
The bed is where I want to be
The duvet wrapping me up so tight
But I'll make do with a cup of tea

Every hour thinking of sleep
Instead of being woken at four
Waiting to count the sheep
But I had two kids, that I adore